Making Friends

By Janine Amos   Illustrated by Annabel Spenceley
Consultant Rachael Underwood

Gareth Stevens Publishing
A WORLD ALMANAC EDUCATION GROUP COMPANY

Please visit our web site at: www.garethstevens.com
For a free color catalog describing Gareth Stevens Publishing's
list of high-quality books and multimedia programs,
call 1-800-542-2595 (USA) or 1-800-387-3178 (Canada).
Gareth Stevens Publishing's fax: (414) 332-3567.

Library of Congress Cataloging-in-Publication Data

Amos, Janine.
    Making friends / by Janine Amos; illustrated by Annabel Spenceley.
        p. cm. — (Courteous kids)
    Includes bibliographical references.
    Summary: Provides examples and tips for making friends, which is
sometimes easy and sometimes hard.
        ISBN 0-8368-3171-3 (lib. bdg.)
        1. Friendship—Juvenile literature. [1. Friendship. 2. Conduct of life.]
    I. Spenceley, Annabel, ill. II. Title.
    BF1533.F8A56 2002
    177'.62—dc21   2002017715

This edition first published in 2002 by
Gareth Stevens Publishing
A World Almanac Education Group Company
330 West Olive Street, Suite 100
Milwaukee, Wisconsin 53212 USA

Gareth Stevens editor: JoAnn Early Macken
Cover Design: Katherine A. Goedheer

This edition © 2002 by Gareth Stevens, Inc. First published by Cherrytree Press,
a subsidiary of Evans Brothers Limited. © 1997 by Cherrytree (a member of the
Evans Group of Publishers), 2A Portman Mansions, Chiltern Street, London
W1M 1LE, United Kingdom. This U.S. edition published under license from
Evans Brothers Limited. Additional end matter © 2002 by Gareth Stevens, Inc.

Printed in the United States of America

1 2 3 4 5 6 7 8 9 06 05 04 03 02

Note to Parents and Teachers

The questions that appear in **boldface** type can be used to initiate
discussion with your children or class. Encourage them to think of
possible answers before continuing with the story.

Tom and Teresa

It's been raining.

Splash! Teresa is jumping in a puddle.

Teresa sees Tom.
"Hi!" says Teresa. "You have boots on, too.
You can jump in the puddles with me."

6

How does Tom feel?

Tom runs toward the puddle.

Splash! He jumps in the puddle with Teresa.

Teresa's mom smiles at them.
"You've made friends," she says.

Danny and Jane

The children are building a house.

Danny is watching.

Danny pushes down the blocks.

The house falls apart.

"Don't do that!" Jane shouts.
"Now we'll have to build the house again."

How do you think Jane feels?
How does Danny feel?

Danny walks away.

Jill follows him.

"You look unhappy," says Jill.

"Did you want to play with the other children?"

Danny nods his head.

"You can if you like," says Jill.
"Tell the children what you want."

"Come with me," says Danny.

Danny and Jill walk over to the blocks.

"I want to play," Danny says to the children.

"Put some blocks here for the roof,"
Jane tells him.

Danny helps Jane build the roof.

They work together.

Jane smiles at Danny.
"You're my friend," she says.

How does Danny feel now?

Sometimes, making friends is easy. You just do something with a new person, and you have fun together. At other times, you don't even know how to start making friends. When you want to join in with others, tell them. You will find a way to play together.

More Books to Read

Don't Need Friends. Carolyn Crimi (Doubleday)

Horace and Morris but Mostly Dolores. James Howe (Atheneum)

The Other Side. Jacqueline Woodson (Putnam)